What's in this book

This book belongs to

_____

奇妙的一星期 A wonderful week

学习内容 Contents

沟通 Communication

说出一星期的日子
Say the days of the week

说出活动名称
Say the names of some activities

生词 New words

☆ 星期一	Monday	
☆ 星期二	Tuesday	
☆ 星期三	Wednesday	
☆ 星期四	Thursday	
☆ 星期五	Friday	
☆ 星期六	Saturday	
☆ 星期日	Sunday	

☆ 看	to look, to see
☆ 看书	to read a book
☆ 朋友	friend
画画	to draw
踢足球	to play football
唱歌	to sing

 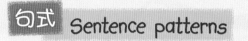

星期三，她看书。
She reads books on Wednesday.

星期四，我们踢足球。
We play football on Thursday.

跨学科学习 Project

计划一周的活动并向朋友说一说
Plan and draw activities for one
week and tell a friend about them

文化 Cultures

表达友情的不同方式
Different ways to show friendship

Get ready

1 Do you think Ling Ling and Elsa are good friends?

2 Do you have good friends?

3 Do you spend time with your friends on Saturdays?

xīng qī yī
星期一

星期一，我们一起上学。

星期二，我们不是朋友。

星期三

星期三，她看书，我画画。

星期四，我们踢足球。

星期五，我们一起唱歌。

xīng qī liù
星期六

xīng qī rì
星期日

星期六、星期日，我们
是好朋友。

Let's think

1 Number the pictures. Act out the story.

2 Suggest ways for Ling Ling and Elsa to be friends again on Tuesday. Draw your ideas in the bubbles.

New words

1 Learn the new words.

星期一
唱歌

星期二
踢足球

星期三
看书

星期四
看书

星期五
画画

星期六
唱歌

星期日

朋友……

2 Write the correct characters to complete the days of the week.

星期一	星期 ___	星期 ___	星期 ___	星期 ___	星期 ___	星期日

听听说说 Listen and say

1 Connect the days.

星期一

星期日

星期二

星期六

星期三

星期五

星期四

2 Write the correct day.

星期 _____

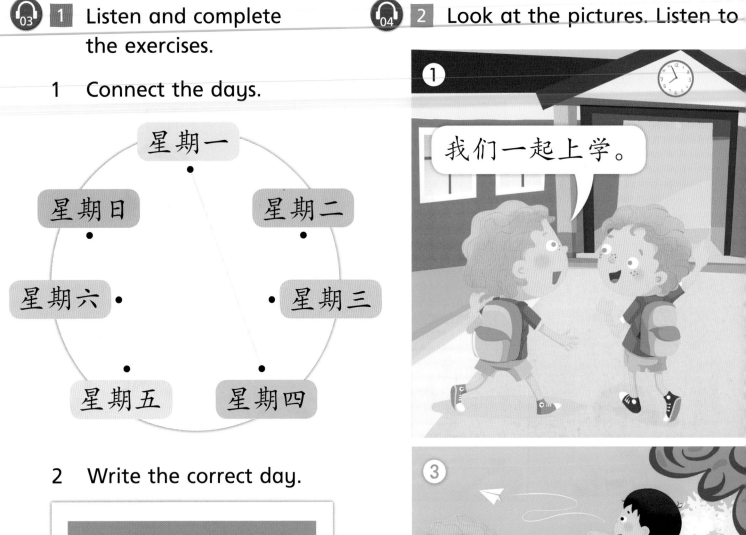

① 我们一起上学。

③ 星期六，伊森画画，浩浩玩飞机。

...tory and say.

星期一，我看书。

星期一，我踢足球。

我们是好朋友！

3 Tick and say the correct sentences.

☐ 星期五，浩浩踢足球。

☐ 星期五，足球踢浩浩。

☐ 我们唱歌星期日。

☐ 星期日，我们唱歌。

Task

Draw your favourite activity for each day of the week. Tell your friend.

星期一，
我……

我喜欢的活动

星期日，
我……

| 星期一 | 星期二 | 星期三 | 星期四 | 星期五 | 星期六 | 星期日 |

Game

Check the calandar. Fill in the blanks with the correct characters.

JANUARY
星期六

FEBRUARY
星期六

MARCH
星期二

APRIL
星期___

MAY
星期___

JUNE
星期___

JULY
星期五

AUGUST
星期___

SEPTEMBER
星期___

OCTOBER
星期___

NOVEMBER
星期___

DECEMBER
星期___

Song

🎧 **Listen and sing.**

一星期，有几天？

一星期，有七天。

一二三，四五六，

星期一到星期六，

没有星期七，

只有星期日。

过了星期日，

再到星期一。

课堂用语 Classroom language

继续。
Continue.

开始。
Start.

轮到你了。
It's your turn.

1 Revise and trace the stroke.

横折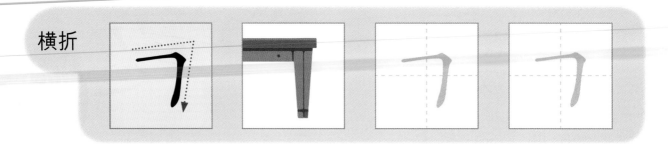

2 Colour 目 in the characters.

盼 相 盯 盾 省

3 How are these characters related to 目? Discuss with your friend.

眉

眼 睛

4 Trace and write the character.

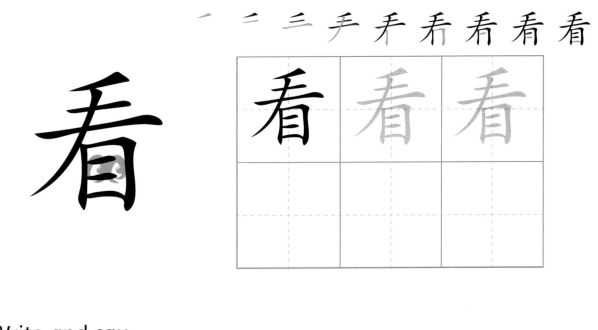

一 二 三 丢 手 看 看 看 看

看

看	看	看

5 Write and say.

爸爸，你 ⬜ ！

汉字小常识 Did you know?

Some characters are made up of left, middle and right components.

Colour the left component red, the middle component blue and the right component green.

谢　　做　　湖　　脚

Cultures

1 Learn and talk about the different ways to show friendship with your friend.

In ancient China, the character for friend 友 was formed by two hands holding each other. Today, people still hold hands to show friendship.

Besides holding hands, there are other ways to show friendship.

2 Colour the bookmarks for your friends.

友 friendship

友 friendship

友 friendship

友 friendship

1 Plan and draw your activities for a week.

2 Show your diary to your friends. Talk about your plan.

星期一，我……

星期二，我……

星期三，我……

星期四，我……

星期五，我……

星期六，我……

星期日，我……

1 Follow the instructions on the cards. Arrange the days from Monday to Sunday and write the letters.

b,

a 星期二

What is the activity?
Say in Chinese.

b 星期一

Read aloud.
星期一

e 星期四

Read aloud.
我们是好朋友。

c 星期六

Trace the character.

看

d 星期日

What are they doing?
Say in Chinese.

f 星期三

Say 'read books' in Chinese.

g 星期五

Write the component.

2 Work with your friend. Colour the stars and the chillies.

Words	说	读	写
星期一	☆	☆	🌶
星期二	☆	☆	🌶
星期三	☆	☆	🌶
星期四	☆	☆	🌶
星期五	☆	☆	🌶
星期六	☆	☆	🌶
星期日	☆	☆	🌶
看	☆	☆	☆
看书	☆	☆	🌶
朋友	☆	☆	🌶

Words and sentences	说	读	写
画画	☆	🌶	🌶
踢足球	☆	🌶	🌶
唱歌	☆	🌶	🌶
星期三，她看书。	☆	☆	🌶
星期四，我们踢足球。	☆	🌶	🌶

Say the days of the week	☆
Say the names of some activities	☆

3 What does your teacher say?

My teacher says ...

21

分享 Sharing

Words I remember

星期一	xīng qī yī	Monday
星期二	xīng qī èr	Tuesday
星期三	xīng qī sān	Wednesday
星期四	xīng qī sì	Thursday
星期五	xīng qī wǔ	Friday
星期六	xīng qī liù	Saturday
星期日	xīng qī rì	Sunday

看	kàn	to look, to see
看书	kàn shū	to read a book
朋友	péng you	friend
画画	huà huà	to draw
踢足球	tī zú qiú	to play football
唱歌	chàng gē	to sing

Other words

| 上学 | shàng xué | to go to school |
| 好 | hǎo | good |

OXFORD
UNIVERSITY PRESS

Oxford University Press is a department of the University of Oxford.
It furthers the University's objective of excellence in research, scholarship,
and education by publishing worldwide. Oxford is a registered trade mark of
Oxford University Press in the UK and in certain other countries

Published in Hong Kong by
Oxford University Press (China) Limited
39th Floor, One Kowloon, 1 Wang Yuen Street, Kowloon Bay,
Hong Kong

First Edition published in 2017

Illustrated by Anne Lee and Wildman

Photographs for reproduction permitted by Dreamstime.com

China National Publications Import & Export (Group) Corporation is an authorized distributor of
Oxford Elementary Chinese.

Please contact content@cnpiec.com.cn or 86-10-65856782

ISBN: 978-0-19-082145-6

10 9 8 7 6 5 4 3